SHERLOCK BONES LOOKS AT THE ENVIRONMENT

Caring for Habitats

Jen Green

WINDMILL BOOKS
New York

Published in 2012 by Windmill Books, LLC
303 Park Avenue South, Suite #1280, New York, NY 10010-3657

First Edition

Editor: Katie Powell
Designer: Stephen Prosser
Maps and Artwork: Peter Bull Art Studio
Sherlock Bones Artwork: Richard Hook
Consultant: Michael Scott, OBE

Library of Congress Cataloging-in-Publication Data

Green, Jen.
Caring for habitats / by Jen Green. — 1st ed.
    p. cm. — (Sherlock Bones looks at the environment)
Includes index.
ISBN 978-1-61533-344-8 (library binding)
1. Habitat (Ecology)—Juvenile literature. 2. Habitat conservation—Juvenile literature. I. Title.
QH541.14.G69 2012
333.95'16—dc22

                            2010047417

Photographs:
Cover © Mike Hill/Getty Images, title page
© Istock, imprint page © Shutterstock, 4 ©
Wayland, 5 © Keren Su/Getty Images, 6 © Cyril
Laubscher/Getty images Mike Hill, 7 © Wayland,
8 © National Geographic/Getty Images, 9 © Mark
Carwardine/ Naturepl, 10 © Wayland, 11 © Franz
Lanting/Corbis, 12 © Wayland /Stockbyte, 13 ©
Mike Hill/Getty Images, 14 © Getty Images, 15 ©
Shutterstock, 16 © Istock, 17 © Ecoscene, 18 ©
Richard Du Toit/Naturepl, 19 © Istock, 20 © Istock,
21 © Pete Oxford/Naturepl, 22 © Istock, 23 ©
Shutterstock, 24 © Michael Scott OBE, 25 ©
Biosphoto.Gunther Michel/Still Pictures, 26 ©
Istock, 27 © Tim Pannell/Corbis, 28 © Chris
James/Still Pictures, 29 © Mark Bolton/Corbis

Manufactured in China

For more great fiction and nonfiction,
go to www.windmillbooks.com

CPSIA Compliance Information: Batch # WAS1102WM:
For Further Information contact Windmill Books, New York, New York at 1-866-478-0556

Contents

Words that appear in **bold** can be
found in the glossary on page 30.

🐾 The Environment Detective, Sherlock Bones, will help you learn about
habitats and how to take care of them. The answers to Sherlock's
questions can be found on page 31.

What Are Habitats?

Plants, animals, and other living things are found almost everywhere on Earth—on land, in seas and lakes, in the air, and even underground. A **habitat** is a particular place where plants and animals live, such as a woodland, river, or coral reef.

Some habitats such as oceans are huge. Others such as a garden pond are tiny. Most habitats are made up of many smaller habitats. For instance, a seashore habitat may contain rock pools, shallow sea, cliffs, and a sandy beach. In a woodland, there may be clumps of a particular tree, clearings, streams, and marshy areas. Each of these small habitats is home to a particular set of living things, called a **community**. Many similar habitats form a much larger area called a **biome**. For instance, many areas of tropical forest with slightly different conditions make up the rain forest biome.

🐾 Study the map below. What are the world's largest biomes?

DETECTIVE WORK

Investigate all the small habitats in your local park or yard. Make a list of mini-habitats such as flower beds, shrubs, grass, a pond, or rock garden. Describe conditions in each habitat. Is it sunny or shady? Exposed or sheltered? Damp, moist, or dry?

This map shows the world's main biomes, or large areas of habitat.

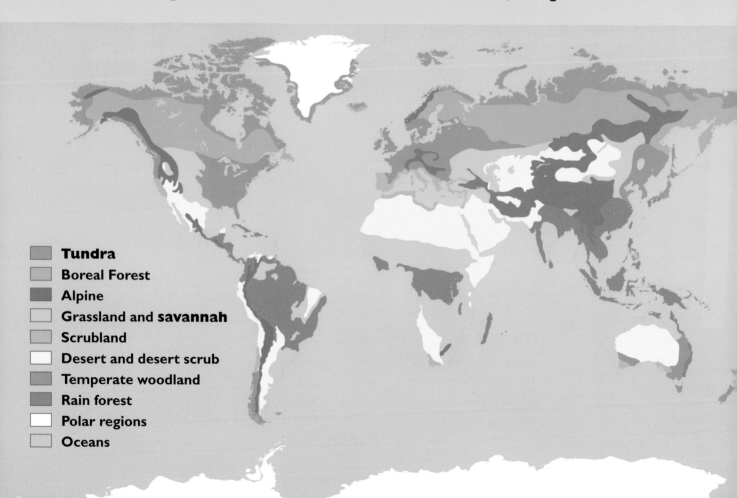

- ■ **Tundra**
- ■ **Boreal Forest**
- ■ **Alpine**
- □ **Grassland and savannah**
- ■ **Scrubland**
- □ **Desert and desert scrub**
- ■ **Temperate woodland**
- ■ **Rain forest**
- □ **Polar regions**
- □ **Oceans**

Giant pandas feed only on a few types of bamboo in certain forests in China. These forests are getting smaller so pandas are in trouble.

Planet Earth is home to a huge number of living things. Scientists have identified more than a million **species** of animals and a quarter of a million land plants. A great many species have yet to be identified. This variety of life is called **biodiversity**.

All living things depend on habitats to provide the conditions they need for survival. However, for centuries people have been changing or destroying many natural habitats, for instance, by cutting down forests or draining marshland. More recently, we have also harmed habitats through **pollution**. Nowadays, most people realize that we need to take better care of nature. This book will explain how everyone can help look after habitats.

ECO-FACTS

Special Requirements

Some living things are able to thrive in many different habitats. For example, red foxes do well in woodlands, fields, and cities. Other species thrive in only one small habitat. The giant panda is found only in the bamboo forests of southwest China. As people have destroyed most of these forests, so pandas have become rare.

How Do Habitats Work?

The living things in a habitat fit together like pieces in a complicated jigsaw puzzle. Plants, animals, fungi, and other **organisms**, together with their surroundings, including the air, soil, and **climate**, form a living system called an **ecosystem**.

Plants, animals, and other living things are **adapted**, or suited, to particular conditions in their habitat, for example, temperature and the amount of moisture. Cactus plants survive in dry places such as deserts by storing water in their stems. However, a cactus would die in a rock pool. Seaweeds are adapted to conditions in rock pools, but would die in a desert.

ECO-FACTS

Evolution

Over time, conditions may change in a habitat. Individual plants or animals that are best suited to the changing conditions are the ones most likely to survive and breed, and so pass on their characteristics to the next generation. Over time, the whole species may change in response to changes in its surroundings. This process is called **evolution**. The idea of evolution was first put forward by the British naturalist, Charles Darwin, in the 1850s.

Predators, such as this falcon, use their sharp beak or talons to catch and kill their **prey.**

Many animals have colors or patterns on their skin, fur, or feathers to help them blend with their **environment**, so it is easier to hunt for food or escape from predators. This is called **camouflage** and it is another example of how living things are adapted to their surroundings.

All living things need food. The plants and animals in a habitat rely on one another for food and other life processes. The connections between them can be shown in diagrams called food chains. Many food chains build up to make a food web. Plants form the base of most food chains. They make their own food using sunlight energy. This process is called **photosynthesis**. Plants provide food for animals called **herbivores**. In turn, herbivores may be eaten by **carnivores**. Animals that hunt others for food are called predators. The top predators in any habitat are at the top of the food chain.

DETECTIVE WORK

Investigate the wildlife in one of the small habitats you found earlier, such as a flower bed or shrub. Think about how each animal is suited to its surroundings, for example, through camouflage. Are the animals you find active by day or night?

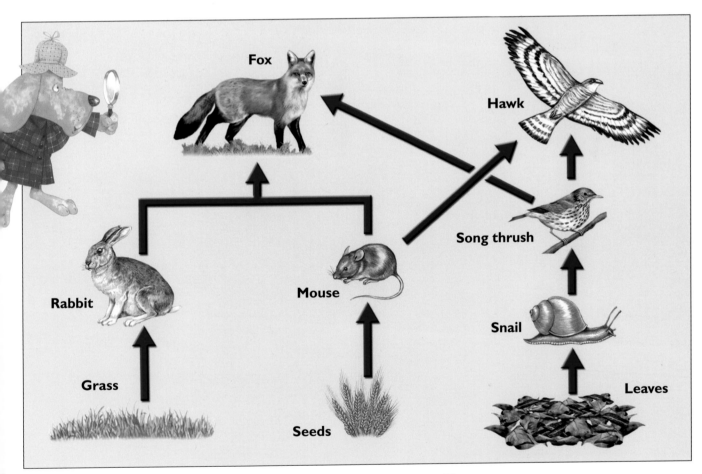

This illustration shows a food web found in a meadow.

🐾 **Which are the top predators in the food web shown here?**

Why Are Habitats Important?

Habitats provide living things with all the conditions they need for survival such as food, water, shelter, and a place to breed. The living things in a habitat are interconnected. If one species dies out, it will affect many other creatures.

Habitats are vital to all living things. Plants provide not only food for animals but also help to keep the air healthy. As plants photosynthesize, they absorb **carbon dioxide** from the air and give out **oxygen**, which animals need to breathe. People need a healthy habitat to survive, too. Plants and animals provide us with essentials such as food, medicine, and clothing.

DETECTIVE WORK

You can find out more about **endangered** species using the Internet. Take a look at the World Wildlife Fund for Nature's web site or the International Union for the Conservation of Nature's web site (IUCN), for details on all endangered species. Can you find out which animals are currently endangered?

Tigers were once found across much of China, India, Indonesia, and into Russia. Now experts believe only about 1,400 tigers are left in India and as few as 40 in China.

If habitats are changed or harmed, the plants and animals there are put at risk. Living things that cannot adapt to changing conditions may become endangered or die out altogether. People are now changing habitats all over the world, which is threatening the survival of many kinds of wildlife. Well-known species, such as the elephant, black rhino, Siberian tiger, orangutan, and mountain gorilla, are all at risk of **extinction**. Since the living things in a habitat form a web of life, the extinction of one species can affect many others.

Extinction is a natural process. Since life began on Earth around 3.8 billion years ago, millions of species have died out naturally. Sometimes thousands of species have died out at one time, in an event called a **mass extinction**. In the past, this has happened because of rapidly changing conditions, such as when huge volcanoes erupted. Now, however, many scientists fear that we are on the brink of another mass extinction, this time caused by people.

The Yangtze dolphin was a rare mammal found only in the Yangtze River, in China. In recent years, people made so many changes to its habitat that the dolphin became endangered. It was declared extinct in 2007.

Mass Extinction

Sixty-five million years ago, dinosaurs, giant **marine** reptiles, and many other species all died out at around the same time, probably because the climate suddenly changed. Experts believe this change was triggered either by an **asteroid** striking the Earth or by a massive volcanic eruption.

Why Are Habitats under Threat?

All over the world, people are taking over areas of natural habitat to build farms, factories, roads, towns, and other developments. Destruction of these wild places is the biggest single threat faced by wildlife.

In 1959, there were 3 billion people on Earth. By 1999, that figure had doubled, to 6 billion. The total is expected to rise to 7 billion by 2012. As human numbers rise, we need more towns to provide homes for everyone, more farmland to grow food, and more mines to produce **minerals** for manufacturing. More land is used for parking lots, airports, roads, and railroads, which leaves less space for wildlife. In poor countries, people cut down trees and forests to get the **fuel** they need to cook and keep warm. But because living things are adapted to their environment, animals, plants, and other wildlife cannot just move elsewhere.

ECO-FACTS

Overhunting

Hunting as well as **habitat loss** presents a serious threat to wildlife. Since prehistoric times, people have hunted animals for meat, fur, or hides. For instance, big cats such as leopards and tigers are killed for their fur. Rhinos and elephants are killed for their horns and ivory tusks, which are made into jewelry and ornaments.

This chart shows you how black rhino numbers have dwindled in Africa since 1960.

KEY
🦏 **1 rhino in chart = 3,000 in the wild**

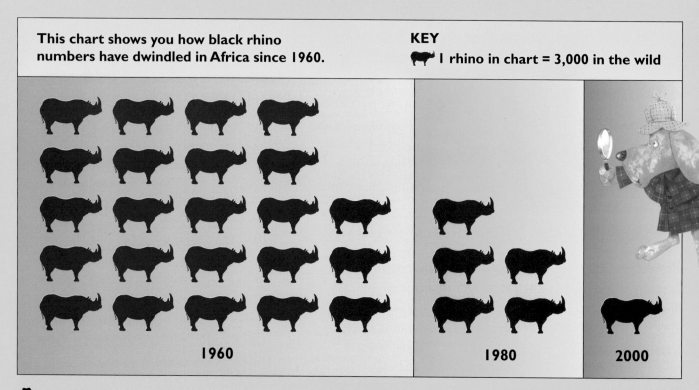

1960

1980

2000

🐾 **Did rhino numbers fall most quickly between 1960 and 1980 or between 1980 and 2000?**

Across the globe, people use very different amounts of the world's resources. In India, 2.5 acres (1 ha) of land is needed to harvest the food and other resources for every person. In western Europe, 12.5 acres (5 ha) is needed, and in the United States, 25 acres (10 ha) is needed for every person.

One type of habitat that is actually growing worldwide is urban habitats, as villages grow into towns, which eventually merge to make large urban areas. A few species, such as opossums, raccoons, magpies, and rodents, are able to thrive alongside humans. Many of the animals that do well in cities have flexible feeding habits, so they are able to take advantage of new food sources, such as scraps of food found in trash cans.

DETECTIVE WORK

Investigate the wildlife that thrives in urban habitats. Look for small creatures such as snails, spiders, worms, and beetles on walls and under stones. Count the number of each species and make a bar graph to record your tally. Which species is most plentiful?

Forest land has been cleared to make way for this development in Rio de Janiero, in Brazil.

How Does Pollution Harm Habitats?

Pollution is a serious hazard that affects many habitats. Some pollution happens naturally, for instance, when a volcano erupts releasing large quantities of ash or lava, but most pollution is caused by people.

Pollution can spread through the air, soil, or water. Waste gases from factories, cities, cars, and power plants pollute the air, producing a poisonous haze called **smog**. Air pollution can also make rain acidic, which harms forests, rivers, and lakes. Waste from mines and factories pollutes the soil, as does all the garbage we throw in dumps and **landfills**. Rivers and lakes may be polluted by chemicals from farms and factories, and **sewage** from cities. Eventually, a lot of river pollution ends up in the sea.

ECO-FACTS

Accident at Sea

In 1989, over 35,000 tons of crude oil accidentally spilled into the sea when the oil tanker *Exxon Valdez* ran aground off Alaska. Half a million seabirds died after their feathers got clogged with oil.

Dead fish show this river is tainted by pollution.

Once in the environment, pollution harms wildlife by entering the food chain. It usually spreads upward from plants or small organisms at the base of the chain. For example, in the oceans, pollution is absorbed by tiny creatures called **plankton**. These are eaten by shrimplike creatures called **copepods**. Fish that eat many copepods can absorb a lot of pollution. Predators such as seals and dolphins, which eat many fish, often absorb very high levels of pollution.

Climate change is a newly-discovered danger related to air pollution. Scientists believe that waste gases, such as carbon dioxide, from factories, cars, and power plants are building up in the atmosphere and trapping more of the sun's heat than normal. This is making temperatures rise worldwide. Climate change is affecting many different habitats. For instance, dry places bordering deserts are becoming even drier. Streams and swamps are drying up, which threatens frogs and other water life. In the polar regions, the ice caps are starting to melt, which is endangering wildlife such as penguins and polar bears.

Polar bears hunt on the Arctic sea ice. If the ice melts, the bears will have nowhere to hunt.

DETECTIVE WORK
Check out the health of your local pond or river. Clear water and wildlife such as insects, fish, and frogs suggest that the habitat is healthy. Litter, foam, or an oily film on the water are signs of pollution, so keep well away from these places.

What Is Being Done to Take Care of Habitats?

Thousands of plants and animals are now at risk because of habitat loss or pollution. Luckily, most people are now aware that nature needs our protection. All over the world, people are taking steps to save wild habitats and wildlife. This work is called **conservation**.

These Greenpeace supporters are drawing attention to the dangers of transporting oil by sea.

Since the 1970s, campaign groups such as Greenpeace and the WWF have been active in conservation. Greenpeace has launched many campaigns to fight pollution and protect rare species such as whales. The WWF has conservation projects in 150 countries. Recently these organizations have warned of the alarming dangers of climate change for wildlife and humans.

ECO-FACTS

Lost Land of the Jaguar

In 2008, a UK television series called *Lost Land of the Jaguar* highlighted the endangered animals, including jaguars and giant otters, in an untouched rain forest in Guyana, in northern South America. The Guyanan government offered to set up a reserve if funds could be raised internationally to pay for the project. The money was found and a million acres (over 400,000 ha) of rain forest is now protected.

In 1872, the world's first national park was set up in the Rocky Mountains of North America. Parks and reserves are now found all over the world, such as here in Australia.

DETECTIVE WORK

Find out more about the national parks in North America using your local library or the Internet. What habitats are being protected? What conservation work is going on?

The best way to protect endangered wildlife such as pandas and black rhinos is to protect the whole habitat in which they live. This can be done by establishing reserves and national parks. Strict rules protect the environment in these areas. For example, mining and building may be banned or kept to a minimum. Visitors are not allowed to disturb animals or pick flowers. In China, 2,300 square miles (6,000 sq. km) of reserves now protect the giant panda. In Africa, with protection, black rhino numbers have risen from 2,410 in 1995 to 4,180 in 2007.

Governments can play a big role in conservation. They can pass laws to outlaw pollution, and introduce planning controls that regulate new development. They can ban the hunting or sale of endangered wildlife and make this practice illegal. Governments can fund conservation work and establish parks and reserves. When tourists visit these reserves to view wildlife, the money they pay is often put back into conservation. This is called **ecotourism**.

Why Are Woods and Forests under Threat?

Woods and forests cover 30 percent of Earth's land surface. They include broad-leaved woodlands that grow in **temperate** regions, and the dark conifer forests of the far north. Tropical rain forests grow closer to the equator. Forests and woodlands are rich in wildlife. Tropical rain forests contain the greatest diversity of any habitat on land.

Fire is a threat in wooded areas. In recent years, major fires have swept through forests in Australia and Southeast Asia after periods of **drought**, which some experts link to climate change.

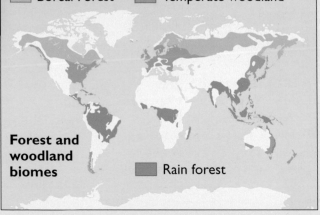

Boreal Forest   Temperate woodland

Forest and woodland biomes

Rain forest

The biggest threat to forest and woodland habitats is **deforestation**. Trees are cut down for their valuable timber, or to burn as fuel. Tropical forests are also cleared to make way for farms or cattle ranches. When this is done, the **vegetation** is often burned. However, forest soil is poor, so farmers and ranchers soon move on to clear a new forest. In the twentieth century, around half of the world's rain forests were destroyed. In 1970, the Amazon rain forest in Brazil covered about 1.54 million square miles (4 million sq. km). In 1990, 1.43 million sq. miles (3.7 million sq. km) were left. That figure had dropped to 1.35 million sq. miles (3.5 million sq. km) by 2000.

🐾 **Did deforestation in the Amazon speed up or slow down between 1990 and 2000?**

DETECTIVE WORK

Investigate the wildlife that lives in your nearest woodland. As you walk around, notice small habitats such as mossy tree stumps, patches of undergrowth, and sunny clearings. Use binoculars to watch for birds in the treetops and a magnifying glass to study small creatures among leaves or on rotten wood.

Rain forest trees such as teak and mahogany are prized for their hardwood timber, which is used to make furniture.

If widespread forest destruction continues, very few forests will be left by 2100. Forest habitats can be saved by setting up national parks and reserves, or by giving local people more rights so that they benefit from looking after the living forest. They can work with foresters to manage their land carefully, only cutting down a few trees so the forest can go on growing, or by replanting seedlings as they go. This is called **sustainable forestry**. There is little disturbance to wildlife and the forest recovers within 20–50 years.

ECO-FACTS

Forests and Climate Change

Forest trees help to maintain the balance of gases in the air by absorbing carbon dioxide and releasing oxygen. This helps to keep Earth's climate stable. When forest land is cleared, the trees that absorbed carbon dioxide are gone, and burning vegetation actually adds to the air pollution that is causing climate change.

How Is the Open Countryside at Risk?

Open countryside is any natural area not covered by trees. Most open countryside is covered by grass. There are two main types of grasslands: temperate grasslands and tropical grasslands, also known as savannah. Wild grasslands are rich in flowering plants, insects, reptiles, birds, and mammals. Large grazing beasts, such as zebras and antelope, roam the African savannah.

Grassland biomes ☐ Grassland and savannah

Tourists pay a fee to view wildlife in the Mala Mala Game Reserve in South Africa. Some of the money is used for conservation.

In temperate regions, reserves have been set up to protect small pockets of wild grassland. The African savannah contains a number of large national parks. Grazing animals such as zebra and wildebeest need to travel huge distances to find water and fresh grazing. Fortunately, many African reserves stretch across national borders, or are linked by strips of wild land that the animals can use.

ECO-FACTS

Organic Farming

Organic farming is a method of farming that doesn't use man-made chemicals. Organic farmers use manure on their fields instead of chemical fertilizers. Animals such as hens and pigs are allowed to roam freely instead of being caged. Organic farming is better for the environment but does require more space, which can put pressure on wild habitats.

Vast expanses of grass once covered the North American prairies and Asian steppes. However, in the last 200 years, huge areas of temperate grasslands have been plowed up to grow crops such as wheat and corn. Until about 50 years ago, European farmland was a patchwork of small fields divided by hedges that sheltered wildlife. But now many of those hedges have been ripped out to make bigger fields where farm machinery can maneuver easily.

Many modern farmers put chemical fertilizers on their fields to increase their harvests. They also spray chemicals called **pesticides** to kill weeds and crop-eating insects. Pesticides harm grassland wildlife by entering the food chain. For example, when mice eat grain that has been sprayed, the poison remains in their bodies. Pesticides can also affect the owls that hunt the mice.

DETECTIVE WORK

Look for organic foods such as meat, eggs, fruit, and vegetables in stores and farmers' markets. Compare the prices of organic and nonorganic foods. Organic food is often a little more expensive, but are you ready to pay more for food grown without using dangerous chemicals?

When fields are sprayed with pesticides, biodiversity is sacrificed in favor of just one plant—the crop.

Can you explain why some owls that live on farmland have been poisoned?

Why Are Rivers and Wetlands in Danger?

Freshwater habitats include streams, rivers, lakes, ponds. and swamps, which shelter fish, frogs, snails, birds, and hundreds of other creatures. All living things need clean, healthy water, but some rivers and wetlands are threatened by habitat loss or pollution.

Rivers, lakes, and other freshwater habitats are incredibly useful to people, as well as wildlife. They provide us with water for drinking, farming, and industry. Fast-flowing rivers and streams are used to produce a type of energy called **hydroelectric power (hydropower)**. Rivers and wetlands provide foods such as fish, and minerals for industry and construction. They are also used for transportation. With all these uses, it is not surprising that many of the world's cities have grown up by rivers and lakes.

🐾 **Power plants by rivers are called hydropower plants. Can you guess why?**

DETECTIVE WORK
Visit the nearest wetland. List the animals you find there and think about how each is suited to its watery habitat. For example, swans and ducks have webbed feet that act as paddles for powerful swimming. Herons have long legs for wading. How are fish and frogs suited for life in water?

Mining can cause serious freshwater pollution. Here, waste from a gold mine pollutes a small creek.

Unfortunately, human use of rivers and wetlands has changed or harmed many freshwater habitats. For instance, rivers are straightened or deepened to make it easier for boats to use them. This destroys riverbank habitats. Marshes are drained to provide land for farming or building. Rivers and streams are dammed to build hydroelectric power plants. The lake that forms behind the dam floods the valley upstream.

Pollution is a serious threat to freshwater habitats. Factories, farms, and towns on the banks of lakes and rivers may cause sewage, fertilizer, waste chemicals, and detergent to enter the water. Sewage and fertilizer can cause tiny water plants called **algae** to multiply very quickly. This removes oxygen from the water, which can kill fish and other water life.

ECO-FACTS

Wetland Conservation

Governments, conservationists, and water authorities are now working hard to improve freshwater habitats. Many nations have signed the Ramsar Convention, an international treaty aimed at improving wetland habitats. By the mid-1900s, European rivers such as the Thames and the Rhine had become heavily polluted and empty of wildlife. Now, these rivers have been cleaned up, and wildlife such as fish have started to return.

The Moremi Game Reserve in the Okavango Delta of Botswana is a huge wetland in southern Africa, which provides a refuge for wildlife.

Why Do Oceans and Coasts Need Our Protection?

Seas and oceans cover more than 70 percent of Earth's surface. Marine habitats include coastal landscapes of many kinds, such as cliffs, mudflats, beaches, lagoons, and coral reefs. Different habitats are also found at various levels in the open ocean, from the sunlit surface waters to the inky-black depths. Each habitat has its own community of living things.

🐾 How could climate change affect the marine habitat shown here?

The Maldives are a group of low-lying islands in the Indian Ocean. The coral reefs here are rich in life.

Like freshwater habitats, seas, oceans, and coasts are also used by people in many different ways. Marine resources include fish and minerals. Fish are a major source of food worldwide. Minerals are dredged from the seafloor, and oil and natural gas are extracted from undersea rocks. For centuries, coastal waters and the open ocean have also been used for transportation. Major cities and ports now line many coasts.

DETECTIVE WORK
A rock pool on the beach is a miniature world containing plants such as seaweed and algae, plant-eaters such as limpets and periwinkles, and carnivores such as whelks (sea snails) and gulls. On a visit to the beach, investigate life in a rock pool. Can you draw a food chain linking the creatures you find?

Unfortunately, our use of marine resources can change or harm coasts and oceans. For example, modern fishing fleets are now so efficient that some types of fish are becoming scarce. Dredging for minerals harms seabed habitats. The drilling of oil has led to major disasters such as the Gulf of Mexico oil spill in 2009.

For centuries, the sea has been used as a dumping ground for all kinds of waste, including highly dangerous nuclear waste. Coastal waters are the most polluted part of the oceans, mainly because waste emptied into rivers ends up in the sea.

Now, scientific evidence shows that climate change caused by air pollution is starting to affect marine habitats. Low-lying coasts and islands are at greater risk of flooding because of rising sea levels. Warming temperatures in the oceans can harm coral reef habitats by killing the coral polyps that build the reefs.

Many nations now set limits called quotas on the amount of fish their fishermen can catch. This should help to save endangered fish.

ECO-FACTS

Marine Conservation

Luckily, help is at hand for marine habitats. Many countries have now signed international agreements—such as the Law of the Sea Treaty—which limit the dumping of waste at sea. Many stretches of coastline have now been made into marine sanctuaries where fishing and other human activities are carefully controlled.

Why Are Remote Habitats at Risk?

The polar regions, mountains, and deserts are the last truly wild places on Earth. The harsh conditions here mean that there are very few **settlements**. Because of this, wildlife is often plentiful. However, not even these remote places are entirely free of problems such as pollution.

The Arctic and Antarctic are the coldest places on Earth. The vast, treeless plains of the tundra lie just south of the Arctic. There are few towns in the Arctic, and none in Antarctica, but even here scientists have found traces of pollution in the air, soil, ice, and water. Mining and drilling for oil has caused pollution in Alaska and Arctic Russia. However, no mining is allowed on Antarctica. Climate change is starting to melt the polar ice, which is affecting wildlife such as seals.

ECO-FACTS

Antarctica

The vast, icy continent of Antarctica was only discovered in the 1820s. By the mid-1900s, many nations had claimed land there, and it looked as if this untouched wilderness would soon be threatened by mining. However, in 1959, all the nations concerned agreed to waive their mining claims on the land, and Antarctica became a wildlife sanctuary.

Limited numbers of tourists are allowed to visit Antarctica but no more than 100 visitors are allowed ashore at any one place at a time.

Tundra | Desert and desert scrub

Polar, tundra, desert, and mountain biomes

Alpine | Polar regions

DETECTIVE WORK

Find out more about wildlife and conservation in Antarctica by typing key words such as environment and conservation + Antarctica into a search engine.

Mountains are known for their clean air and wild, untouched scenery. They also contain **natural resources** such as forests, minerals, and fast-flowing rivers. Deforestation, mining, dam-building, and ski developments have harmed mountain habitats in some areas. Mountains are popular places to go on vacation, but tourism can cause problems. Visitors may drop litter or disturb shy mountain animals, and their cars cause pollution. Cars are banned in some resorts, for example, in the Swiss Alps.

Deserts cover about a quarter of Earth's surface. They are home to hardy plants and animals that can withstand very dry conditions. However, these fragile habitats are easily damaged by people. In the late 1900s, drilling for oil in deserts such as Arabia caused pollution. Now scientists fear deserts are expanding as dry areas on their borders are regularly hit by drought. Core desert areas are getting even hotter and harsher for life.

The oryx is a desert antelope from Arabia. By the 1970s, it was almost extinct but the last animals were captured and bred in zoos. A small herd has now been returned to the wild.

How Can We Help to Take Care of Habitats?

Habitats such as rain forests and the savannah may be far away from where you live, but there are things we can all do to protect wild places. If everyone does even a little to protect nature, it can make a big difference to habitats and wildlife both at home and abroad.

Doing your part for the environment helps to keep habitats such as the seashore clean and healthy for plants and animals to use and for people to enjoy.

The energy we use at home is produced by power plants that give off the gases that are causing climate change. Using energy more carefully reduces air pollution. For instance, why not switch off lights, computers, and other machines when you are not using them? Cars also cause air pollution. Walk, cycle, or use public transportation instead of going by car whenever you can.

DETECTIVE WORK

Follow the work of your favorite conservation group by logging onto their web site. Many groups have schemes that allow you to sponsor your favorite animal. You could do a sponsored swim, walk, or bicycle ride to raise money for conservation.

Ask your teacher if you can organize a class trip to clean up litter on the beach or in the countryside.

Wasting water at home adds to the pressure on watery habitats such as streams, rivers, and lakes. Save water by turning off dripping faucets and taking a short shower instead of a bath. Trees in distant forests are cut down to provide the paper and cardboard we use at home. Save trees by writing on both sides of paper and buying products made from recycled paper or card.

Take care of local habitats by taking home your own litter. Don't pick wild plants. If you pick up animals to study them, treat them gently and put them back when you are finished. In the national parks, always follow the park rules, and keep to the paths to avoid trampling wild plants. On vacation, take care not to disturb wildlife, such as birds breeding on beaches. Don't buy souvenirs made from animal products, such as shells, coral, or ivory.

ECO-FACTS

Litter and Recycling

Litter harms wild habitats and can trap or injure animals. Most of the litter you see on streets or in the countryside consists of cans, bottles, candy wrappers, paper, or cardboard packaging for food and drinks. All of these materials are made with **raw materials** found in the natural world. Recycling glass, cans, and other packaging helps to save materials and natural habitats.

Your Project

If you've done the detective work and answered Sherlock's questions, you now know a lot about habitats and conservation. Investigate further by doing your own project. You could choose from the following ideas.

Practical Action

Design a mini-reserve for a corner of the yard or school grounds. First, think about the space that is available. Your reserve could be large enough for several small habitats, such as shrubs and a pond or rock garden, or small enough to fit in a window box. It could include a patch of wild flowers to attract bees and butterflies. A rock garden or a small pile of logs will shelter beetles, spiders, and wood lice. A small pond will provide a home for frogs, newts, and dragonflies. You might add a bird table or hanging bird feeder. Draw a map of the mini-reserve. When you are finished, see if you can convince your parents or teacher to help you make it a reality!

Topics to Investigate

- Find out as much as you can about one particular habitat or biome, either in your area or another state or country. What are conditions like there? How are living things suited to their surroundings? Can you draw a food web linking wildlife in the ecosystem?
- Find out all you can about a particular national park, nature reserve, or conservation project, either in your area or another state or country. Investigate the threats to the environment and the conservation work that goes on there. Or you could compare two conservation areas in different countries. One could be a large park and the other a small nature reserve.

Your local library and the Internet can provide all kinds of information. Try the web sites listed on page 31. When you have gathered the information, you might like to present it using one of the ideas on page 29.

These children are taking care of a mini-reserve in their school grounds.

Project Presentation

- Write a story or poem about the habitat you have chosen from the perspective of an animal living there. You might choose an endangered species such as an orangutan, blue whale, or mountain gorilla.

- Imagine you are writing a magazine article or making a television documentary about the habitat. Plan a structure showing the main points you want to make.

- People living in an environment have different attitudes to nature, especially when their work is involved. You could write about the habitat from the point of view of one or two of the following: a farmer, a park ranger, a wildlife expert, a vacationer, an environmental campaigner, a factory owner, or a fisherman.

Putting out food for birds helps them survive, particularly in harsh winter weather.

🐾 **Sherlock has found out about the habitats of his ancestor, the wolf. Wolves live in many different habitats, including conifer forests, the tundra, grasslands, mountains, and deserts.**

Glossary

adapted Suited to the environment.

algae Tiny plants that grow in water or damp places.

asteroid A large mass of rock from space.

biodiversity The variety of life in the world or in a habitat.

biome A habitat covering a large area, such as a rain forest or the tundra.

camouflage The colors or markings on an animal's skin that match its habitat.

carbon dioxide A gas absorbed by plants and given off by animals as they breathe. It is also produced when fuels are burned.

carnivore An animal that eats meat.

climate The long-term weather conditions in a region.

climate change Any long-term significant change in the weather patterns of an area.

community All the living things found in a particular environment.

conservation Work done to protect the natural world.

copepod A tiny, shrimplike animal found in the ocean.

deforestation When forest land is cleared of trees.

drought A period without rain.

ecosystem A web of life made up of all the living things in a habitat together with the soil, air, and conditions such as climate.

ecotourism A form of tourism that does little damage to the environment; the money from it helps conservation.

endangered At risk of becoming extinct.

environment The surroundings in which people or wildlife live.

evolution When a species changes over time in response to conditions in the environment.

extinction When a species dies out completely.

fuel A substance that can be burned or used up to produce energy.

habitat A place where particular types of plants and animals live, such as a desert or coral reef.

habitat loss The result of people destroying areas of wild habitat.

herbivore An animal that eats plants.

hydroelectric power (hydropower) Energy produced from fast-flowing water.

landfill A hole in the ground in which garbage is dumped.

marine To do with the sea.

mass extinction When a very large number of species die out at around the same time.

mineral A nonliving natural substance.

natural resources Resources that are found in nature.

organic farming A method of farming without using man-made chemicals, such as pesticides.

organism A living thing. Plants, animals, and fungi are major groups of organisms.

oxygen A gas that makes up one-fifth of Earth's atmosphere, which animals use to breathe.

pesticide A chemical used to kill weeds, insects, or fungi that harm crops.

photosynthesis The process by which plants live and grow using sunlight energy and water. Plants give off oxygen during photosynthesis.

plankton A tiny organism found in the sea.

pollution Any harmful substances that damage the environment.

predator An animal that hunts other animals for food.

prey An animal that becomes the food of a hunter.

raw material A natural substance that is used in manufacturing.

savannah A tropical grassland.

settlement A place where people live, such as a village, town, or city.

sewage Dirty water from homes, containing chemicals and human waste.

smog A poisonous haze that forms when air pollution reacts with sunlight.

species A type of plant or animal, such as the black rhino.

sustainable forestry A type of forestry that involves harvesting some timber without lasting harm to the forest.

temperate An area that has mild temperatures.

tundra The treeless lowlands of the far north that are permanently frozen.

vegetation Plants found in a particular area or habitat.

Answers

🐾 **Page 4:** The oceans are the world's largest biome. The boreal forest (northern conifer forests) is the largest biome on land.

🐾 **Page 7:** Red foxes and hawks are the top predators in the food web shown.

🐾 **Page 10:** In the 20 years between 1960 and 1980, rhino numbers fell by 55,000. Between 1980 and 2000, they fell by 12,000, so numbers fell more steeply during the earlier period when rhinos were more plentiful.

🐾 **Page 16:** In the 20 years between 1970 and 1990, 0.11 million sq. miles (0.3 million sq. km) of rain forest was lost. Between 1990 and 2000, 0.08 million sq. miles (0.2 million sq. km) were lost in just ten years, so deforestation sped up between 1990 and 2000.

🐾 **Page 19:** Owls that eat many mice that have fed on poisoned grain absorb a lot of poison.

🐾 **Page 20:** Hydropower is hydroelectric power.

🐾 **Page 22:** Warming ocean temperatures are harming coral reefs, and rising sea levels could one day swamp low-lying islands, such as the Maldives.

Further Reading and Web Sites

Books

Earth Issues: Wildlife in Danger
by Valerie Bodden
(Creative Education, 2010)

Eye to Eye with Endangered Habitats
by Precious McKenzie
(Rourke Publishing, 2010)

Protecting Our Planet: Habitats and Wildlife in Danger
by Sarah Levete
(Crabtree Publishing, 2010)

Web Sites

For Web resources related to the subject of this book, go to: http://www.windmillbooks.com/weblinks and select this book's title.

Index

The numbers in **bold** refer to pictures.